DAILY LIFE IN US HISTORY

LIFE DURING THE GREAT DEPRESSION

by Wendy H. Lanier

Content Consultant
Jonathan Bean
Professor of History
Southern Illinois University

Core Library

An Imprint of Abdo Publishing
www.abdopublishing.com

www.abdopublishing.com

Published by Abdo Publishing, a division of ABDO, PO Box 398166, Minneapolis, Minnesota 55439. Copyright © 2015 by Abdo Consulting Group, Inc. International copyrights reserved in all countries. No part of this book may be reproduced in any form without written permission from the publisher. Core Library™ is a trademark and logo of Abdo Publishing.

Printed in the United States of America, North Mankato, Minnesota
092014
012015

Cover Photo: AP Images
Interior Photos: AP Images, 1, 11, 15, 18, 20, 31, 45; Frigidaire/AP Images, 4; Corbis, 6, 26, 42; Red Line Editorial, 10, 24; Underwood & Underwood/Corbis, 12; Hulton-Deutsch Collection/Corbis, 28; Bettmann/Corbis, 34; H. Armstrong Roberts/ClassicStock/Corbis, 37; Kirn Vintage Stock/Corbis, 39

Editor: Mirella Miller
Series Designer: Becky Daum

Library of Congress Control Number: 2014944229

Cataloging-in-Publication Data
Lanier, Wendy H.
 Life during the Great Depression / Wendy H. Lanier.
   p. cm. -- (Daily life in US history)
 ISBN 978-1-62403-626-2 (lib. bdg.)
 Includes bibliographical references and index.
 1. Depressions--1929--United States--Social aspects--Juvenile literature. 2. Stock Market Crash, 1929--Social aspects--Juvenile literature. 3. United States--Economic conditions--1918-1945--Juvenile literature. 4. Europe--Economic conditions--1918-1945--Juvenile literature. I. Title.
 338.5--dc23
                                                2014944229

CONTENTS

CHAPTER ONE

NOSE DIVE

Can you imagine waiting in line for food or a place to sleep? Or dust storms that buried your home in dirt? These were common occurrences during the Great Depression. In 1928 a growing number of Americans were wealthy and successful. More people had money to buy cars and modern appliances. When they did not have cash available, they bought on credit. On the surface, it seemed the United States'

Working families in the late 1920s were able to buy items once considered luxuries, such as refrigerators, when buying on credit.

In the late 1920s, many farmers were no longer making money.

future was bright and prosperous. But many factors would soon lead to the crash of the US economy.

For one, unemployment was becoming a problem. Factories were creating new products faster and better than ever before. New manufacturing methods required skilled labor. Workers who were not skilled lost their jobs. In some parts of the country, unemployment slowly began to rise.

US farmers were suffering too. Farmers had exported many of their products to Europe during

World War I (1914–1918). This had provided them with extra profit. Some farmers had borrowed money during the war to buy more land, hoping to make even more money. But after the war, Europe no longer needed US goods. Prices on farm products began to drop. Between 1920 and 1921, prices fell by 40 percent. Many farmers could not pay their loans and lost their land.

Buying and Selling Stocks

The stock market crash in 1929 showed the financial problems of the United States. Buying and selling on the stock market increased during the 1920s. With so many people looking for ways to invest their money, businesses saw an opportunity. Big companies began selling stocks in their businesses. A stock is a share of the value of a company. People who bought stocks were called investors or shareholders. They hoped to make a profit on their investments by selling them for more than they had paid.

The Average American

Investors felt the effects of the stock market crash firsthand. But the effects slowly made their way to other Americans too. Business owners had to lay off workers, cut back on production, reduce wages, and cut the prices they charged for their goods. Even with lower prices, Americans did not buy as much as before. Many Americans lost their jobs. Banks were now short on cash and could not give money out to people who were storing it there. People no longer trusted banks, which caused many banks to close. In order to save the money they had, families bought less.

Shareholders could profit from their investment in two ways. A company that made money paid out part of its profits to its shareholders. Another way to make a profit was for investors to buy stock and sell it for more than the purchase price. Soon investors stopped worrying about whether a company was successful enough to make money in the long run. They only cared about the current stock price.

Black Tuesday

The buying and selling of stocks reached its peak in late September. Then stock prices began to fall. Soon the stock market was in a deep slide. Eventually the stock market hit an all-time low on October 29, 1929. More than 16.4 million shares were sold that day. Americans lost approximately $25 billion. The day became known as Black Tuesday.

The Stock Market Crash

Many investors during the 1920s did not know a lot about the stock market. They did not understand that buying stock meant taking risks. A few dishonest investors agreed to sell stocks to each other at high prices. This drove the price of some stocks up, making it more expensive for new investors. The dishonest investors would then sell their stocks for a profit. The value of the stock eventually went down. People began to sell their stocks quickly. This created panic among investors, which led to the Black Tuesday crash.

Smoot-Hawley Tariff Act

While the country was still recovering from Black Tuesday, another event caused more trouble.

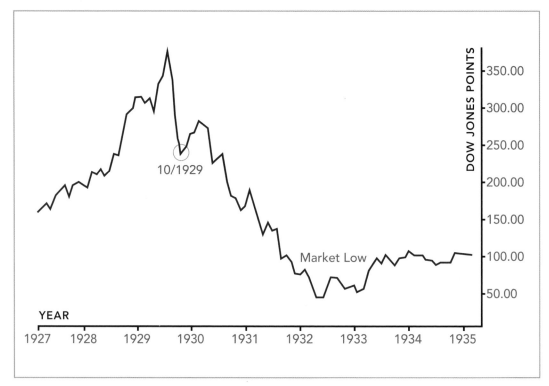

Stock Market Prices
The graph shows stock market activity beginning in 1927. How would you describe the strength of the stock market before October 1929? What were stock market prices after October 1929? After reading this chapter, how do you think the stock market crash affected Americans' daily life?

Congress passed the Smoot-Hawley Tariff Act in 1930. This act placed high taxes on products imported to the United States. It was supposed to protect US manufacturing and farm production. Instead it brought a stop to US imports and exports because other nations passed similar laws to keep

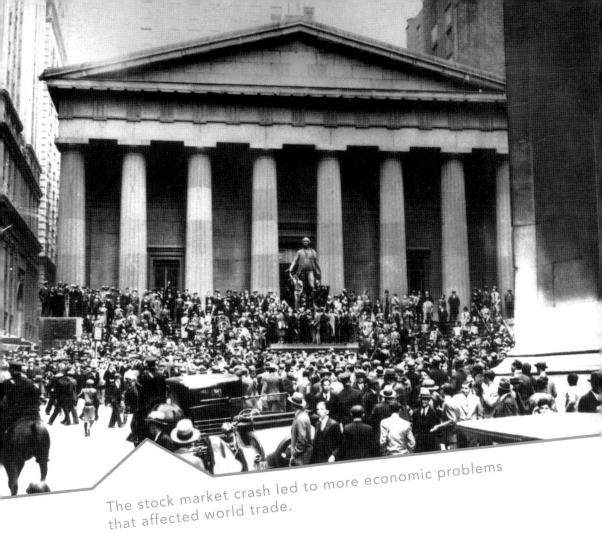

The stock market crash led to more economic problems that affected world trade.

US products out. The law sparked a trade war that hurt all nations. World trade dropped by more than 50 percent after the act was passed. Soon the whole world was facing a financial crisis.

UNEMPLOYED
BUY
APPLES
5 C. EACH

CHAPTER TWO

FROM BAD TO WORSE

B y 1932 the United States was in the middle of the Great Depression. This would be the longest economic slump of the 1900s. As financial experts had warned, many factories shut down as a result of the bad economy. Unemployment rose from 8.7 percent in 1930 to 23.6 percent by 1932.

There were problems for those who managed to keep their jobs too. Workers often had to take

Many people who were unemployed did anything they could to make a little money, including selling fruit on the streets.

less pay to stay employed. Children in low-income families sometimes dropped out of school to work. Any money a family made went toward food and paying bills.

The loss of jobs and wages led many Americans to be careful about their spending. They stopped buying anything but the most necessary items. Less demand for products caused more factories to close. Even more people lost their jobs. Many people could no longer pay for the items they had bought on credit. Sometimes a family's car or new stove was taken away. Some families lost their homes.

Organized Crime

In 1920 the government banned the sale of alcohol. Soon after, crime became an organized business. Big-city gangs took over the production and sale of alcohol. Police tried to stop the gangs, but they were too powerful. The Federal Bureau of Investigation was in charge of finding these gangs and prosecuting them.

Farmers in the Depression

Farmers who still owned their farms managed

A dust cloud picks up dirt from a road in Oklahoma.

better than others during the Depression. They could live off their own produce. Families traded what they did not eat for other items. It was just enough to survive.

But farmers on the Great Plains faced a tougher situation. The United States suffered from one of history's worst droughts during the 1930s. Southwestern states were especially affected. Farmers had planted the same crops year after year. This damaged the soil and left nothing to keep the topsoil in place. When the wind blew, it sent dust

Tales of the Dust Bowl

Charles Briscoe was a young man living in the Dust Bowl. On March 4, 1935, Briscoe was riding in a car being pulled by a truck. The bright day suddenly turned dark with dust clouds. After the truck stopped, Briscoe had to feel his way to it. Briscoe's mother put a lamp in the window so he could find his way home. Dust clouds could stay for days. Wet sheets were hung over each family member's bed at night. These sheets kept dust out of their lungs.

swirling through the air. Soon the land was useless for farming. The Southwestern states suffering from the drought became known as the Dust Bowl. These states included Oklahoma, Texas, Nebraska, Kansas, and Colorado.

Growing Hungry

The number of people across the country without jobs and homes grew. Many Americans did what they could to survive. Sometimes families were forced to take donations. Soup kitchens sprang up all over the country. Those who were poor and hungry could stop at a soup kitchen. People waited in lines to be served soup and bread. One soup kitchen in Detroit, Michigan, served between 1,500 and 3,000 people each day.

President Hoover

Herbert Hoover was president from 1929 to 1933. He did not believe the Depression could be fixed solely by government action. He worried government help would destroy the United States' strong spirit. He believed the economic depression would eventually fix itself.

President Hoover's refusal to do more angered many Americans. In 1928 voters had great faith in Hoover's abilities to fix the economy. They gave him credit for the success of the 1920s. But when the Depression began, Americans blamed Hoover. With nowhere else to go, homeless people began building shacks in empty lots across the country. People called the little shack towns "Hoovervilles" after the president. Many Hoovervilles were built near rivers for a water source. Some towns had vegetable gardens. But many Hoovervilles were dirty and unorganized.

Hooverville shacks were made of cardboard, tar paper, glass, tin, and anything else people could find.

In 1932 veterans of World War I asked the government to pay their bonuses earlier than the 1945 due date. The bonuses were for their service during the war. Many veterans marched in Washington, DC in support of the Bonus Bill. When Congress rejected the Bonus Bill, Americans were ready for change. They hoped electing Franklin Delano Roosevelt would be the change the country needed.

Many Americans were left with very little during the Great Depression. Some people moved from place to place in search of paying work. A song written by a migrant worker in 1938 describes the feelings of many Americans during the Depression era:

> We go around all dress in rags
>
> While the rest of the world goes neat,
>
> And we have to be satisfied
>
> With half enough to eat.
>
> We have to live in lean-tos.
>
> Or else we live in a tent,
>
> For when we buy our bread and beans
>
> There's nothing left for the rent. . . .

Source: Lester Hunter. *"I'd Rather Not Be on Relief."* Library of Congress. *Library of Congress*, 1938. Web. Accessed July 30, 2014.

Back It Up

The author of this song is using evidence to support a point. Write a paragraph describing the point the author is making. Then write down two or three pieces of evidence the author uses to make the point.

CHAPTER THREE

A NEW DEAL

In the months following President Roosevelt's election, problems with the banking industry grew. More and more banks were closing. People hurried to banks to withdraw all of their cash. This made the banking crisis worse. By March 1933, the nation's banking system had collapsed.

President Roosevelt was inaugurated on Saturday, March 4, 1933. He declared March 6 a national bank

One of the first actions President Roosevelt took in office was reassuring the nation about the bank problems via a radio broadcast.

holiday and called Congress into a special session. Their first task was to deal with the bank crisis. Congress passed the Emergency Banking Act of 1933 that week. The law allowed the government to inspect and reorganize all national banks.

On March 12, 1933, President Roosevelt addressed the nation in the first of many radio broadcasts known as fireside chats. Many Americans gathered around their radios to listen. President Roosevelt explained what banking experts had been doing all week. He also took time to carefully explain how banks work. President Roosevelt

PERSPECTIVES

African Americans in the Depression

Life was extra hard for African Americans. Slavery was illegal, but they still faced racism and discrimination. This made it hard to find jobs. African-American communities often found creative ways to survive. Rent parties began in Harlem, New York, and quickly spread to other parts of the country. Guests paid 15 cents for an evening of food and fun, while the host raised enough money to pay rent.

promised Americans the banks would be safe when they reopened. The broadcast reassured many Americans. Within a few days, more Americans were putting money back into the banks.

New Deal Programs

Over the next three months, President Roosevelt created a series of government agencies known as New Deal programs. Minimum wages and five-day workweeks were part of the New Deal. President Roosevelt also planned to control the stock market and provide grants to farmers and the poor.

The New Deal agencies gave the US government power to control businesses, state governments, and the economy. Some Americans worried it gave the government too much power. In 1935 and 1936, the US Supreme Court declared some programs unlawful.

The Second New Deal

Some New Deal programs continued. Other programs were created as part of the Second New

Program	Acronym	Year	Significance
Civil Works Administration	CWA	1933	Provided jobs at $15/week to 4 million workers.
Civilian Conservation Corps	CCC	1933	Sent 250,000 young men to work camps to perform restoration and conservation tasks.
Federal Emergency Relief Act	FERA	1933	Distributed millions of dollars of direct aid to unemployed workers.
National Youth Administration	NYA	1935	Provided part-time employment to more than 2 million college and high school students.
Securities and Exchange Commission	SEC	1934	Regulated the stock market.
Works Progress Administration	WPA	1935	Employed 8.5 million workers in construction, arts, theater, and literary projects.

New Deal Programs

Most Americans called the New Deal programs by their initials. Choose one of the programs from the chart. Find out what the program was supposed to do. Was the program effective during the Depression? How did it help Americans in their daily lives? Does the program still exist?

Deal (1935–1938). The Securities and Exchange Commission (SEC) controlled the stock market and protected investors. The Works Progress Administration (WPA) created jobs when it approved public building projects. Unemployed and retired workers received help from the Social Security Act. Social Security still exists today as the largest program in the US government.

Clothing, Food, and Repairs

Despite Roosevelt's efforts, for most of the 1930s there was only slight improvement in the economy. The new programs put many people back to work. But daily life was still tough. Americans were encouraged to reuse, mend, and make do with items they had. Having little money to spend meant Americans learned to make what they needed on their own.

Women knitted and sewed clothing at home rather than buying it new. Dresses were often made out of chicken feed sacks. Americans were careful not to throw things away. An old object could be made into something useful. Towels were mended or cut up for washcloths. Old sheets were cut into strips that could be woven into blankets.

Families had to be creative with the items they had during the Great Depression.

People made their groceries go further by inventing recipes that did not use butter or eggs. Both items were hard to get in the Depression years. Sometimes they added fillers such as bread or crackers to their recipes. Powdered milk, dried beans, and potatoes were common in many households. These items were inexpensive and easier to find.

Franklin Delano Roosevelt was elected president in 1932 in the middle of the Great Depression. He had a large task ahead of him to fix the country's economy. His first inaugural address touched on how the country could overcome the problem:

> *This great Nation will endure, as it has endured, will revive and will prosper.*
>
> *So, first of all, let me assert my firm belief that the only thing we have to fear is fear itself—nameless, unreasoning, unjustified terror which paralyzes needed efforts to convert retreat into advance. In every dark hour of our national life, a leadership of frankness and of vigor has met with that understanding and support of the people themselves which is essential to victory. And I am convinced that you will again give that support to leadership in these critical days.*
>
> Source: Franklin Delano Roosevelt. "First Inaugural Address." American Rhetoric. American Rhetoric, March 3, 1933. Web. Accessed July 30, 2014.

Changing Minds

Take a position on President Roosevelt's inauguration speech. Imagine your best friend has the opposite opinion. Write a blog post trying to change your friend's mind. Make sure you explain your opinion and your reasons for it. Include facts and details that support your reasons.

CHAPTER FOUR

ESCAPING THE DEPRESSION

The Depression affected some Americans more than others. But nearly everyone felt the burden of trying to survive in hard economic times. The Depression made people tighten their wallets and make do with less. It also caused them to look for new ways to forget their troubles.

Actors Fred Astaire and Ginger Rogers helped make dancing a popular pastime through their movies.

At the Movies

Many movies during the Great Depression were lighthearted and full of music. Movies often told rags-to-riches stories, in which people fell on hard times but turned their lives around. These stories offered Americans an escape from the worries of daily life and a sense of possibility.

Many movies also featured dancing and singing. Director Busby Berkeley created musicals with beautiful costumes and elaborate dance numbers. Dance studios became common. Everyone wanted to learn to dance like Fred Astaire and Ginger Rogers.

PERSPECTIVES
Celebrity Criminals

Newspapers and movies of the 1930s turned criminals into romantic figures. Bonnie Parker and Clyde Barrow were famous murderers. John Dillinger was a gangster and bank robber. He was considered the most dangerous man of his time. Al Capone was a famous mob boss from Chicago who often made contributions to charities.

Sometimes dance marathons went on for days.

Marathon Dancing

The dance craze started by Fred Astaire and Ginger Rogers made marathon dancing a popular contest in cities across the country. During these contests, dancers danced for as long as they could. Contestants paid a small fee to enter in hopes of winning a cash prize. Because many contestants were unemployed, the free food and shelter provided by the contests were also big draws.

The WPA

The Works Progress Administration (WPA) put many people to work building parks, hospitals, roads, and public buildings. But it also funded cultural projects involving art, music, writing, and theater. Young artists taught art classes and helped set up community art centers. Musicians taught classes and performed concerts. Young actors wrote, produced, and performed plays across the country. Writers were hired to write books about each state. They also collected oral histories and folklore to preserve US history.

Radio Programs

In the early 1930s, radios became smaller and less expensive. Most families owned a radio by 1933. Families would gather around the radio at night to listen to crime dramas, comedies, or music.

Golfing and Other Sports

Despite having little money to spend, people stayed active during the Depression. Up until the Depression, golf had mostly been a wealthy man's game. But as private golf clubs lost members, many courses went public. A small fee allowed access to the course for a day of play. The WPA was soon building more public golf courses across the country.

In 1932 the winter Olympics were held in Lake Placid, New York. Newscasters reported the events by radio. Many families sat around their radios at night to hear the results. Snow skiing quickly became a popular winter sport after the Olympics were finished.

FURTHER EVIDENCE

There is quite a bit of information about culture and entertainment during the Depression in Chapter Four. What is the main point of this chapter? What key evidence supports this point? Go to the article about entertainment at the website below. Find a quote from the website that supports the chapter's main point. Does the quote support an existing piece of evidence in the chapter? Or does it add a new one?

Having Fun during the Great Depression
www.mycorelibrary.com/great-depression

Match
1. bronze
2. Bronz Age
3. forge
4. Iron Age
5. Metel Age
6. prehistoric
7. picture writing
8. ore

CHILDREN IN THE DEPRESSION

Adults were not the only ones who tried to escape from the worries of the Depression. Children did too. For many students, school was a place to stay busy and productive. But many schools closed during the Depression. Fewer people were able to pay their taxes. This meant fewer funds were available to hire teachers or buy supplies.

Depression-era students were expected to work on their lessons while the teacher taught other grades.

In many communities, students were expected to buy their own supplies and books. Many children dropped out of school because their families had no money to buy clothes or supplies. Schools in rural areas suffered the most from the lack of funds. The schools had a single teacher for all grade levels. Often older students helped the younger children with their work.

African-American Schools

In most areas of the United States, African-American children went to separate schools from white students. African-American schools received even less funding than white schools. Teachers were often paid less too. They were expected to make do with hand-me-down books and supplies. The supplies were usually well-worn. This meant books were often missing pages.

The main focus of most classrooms during the 1930s was on reading.

Reading Books

Many children learned to read using *Dick and Jane* readers. These books were first introduced in 1927. Many children also enjoyed reading for fun. Dr. Seuss's first book, *And to Think That I Saw It on Mulberry Street*, was a big hit in 1937. Nancy Drew mystery books were popular with girls too.

Coming of Age

Children were greatly affected by the Depression. Those from poor families often quit school to work. They had to help support their families from a young age. Many young men from poor families went to work for the Civilian Conservation Corps (CCC). The program provided work planting trees, a place to stay, and a small income. Most of the money they earned went back to their families. In middle- and upper-class families, young people were more likely to stay in school. High school attendance was high. Some students continued their studies through college and graduate school. With so few jobs available, there was little else to do.

Toys and Games

Because most families did not have a lot of money, many toys from the Depression were homemade. Scooters and race cars were often made from orange crates. Wheels from roller skates were attached to the bottom of the crates. Bicycles were popular, but a new bike was expensive. Most bikes were bought used. Many dolls during the Depression were made from rags sewn together. Children

Marbles were another popular game that many kids could play outside.

decorated the faces with buttons and other fabric scraps.

Although homemade toys were common, a number of store-bought toys became instant favorites. Many popular board games, including Scrabble, Monopoly, and backgammon, were first introduced in the 1930s. They quickly became hits with children and adults. Lincoln Logs and Tinker Toys

Entering the War

President Roosevelt tried to put people back to work with his New Deal programs. But by 1938, approximately 20 percent of the population was still unemployed. By 1938, many Americans turned against the New Deal because it had failed to quickly bring recovery. Then German dictator Adolf Hitler invaded Poland in 1939. Soon there was war across Europe. The United States began sending supplies and war materials to help the countries fighting Hitler. US factories began producing war goods. More and more factory jobs were added across the country. By the time the United States entered World War II in 1941, the Great Depression was officially over.

first appeared during the Depression too. Those who were lucky enough to get store-bought toys usually took good care of them. Even children knew they were a luxury.

Whether there were toys or not, the children of the Depression found ways to have fun. Pretend play, hide-and-seek, and tag were all popular games that could include the entire neighborhood.

The End of the Depression

The economic hard times created by the Great Depression made an impact on both children and adults. It was a time of pinching pennies and making do. The Depression created a generation of Americans with a strong attitude. It would serve them well in the dark days ahead. World War II (1939–1945) was looming on the horizon. The United States was about to be put to a different kind of test.

EXPLORE ONLINE

The focus of Chapter Five is school and play during the Great Depression. The website below also focuses on toys from the 1930s. As you know, every source is different. How is the information given in the website different from the information in this chapter? What information is the same? How do the two sources present information differently? What can you learn from this website?

Popular Toys from the 1930s
www.mycorelibrary.com/great-depression

Andy is a 12-year-old boy. His father is having a hard time keeping a job. To make sure Andy doesn't go hungry, his parents send him to live with his grandparents on their farm. Andy is expected to help his grandparents while he is there.

6:00 a.m.
Andy gets up to help round up the cows for milking. While his grandfather and uncle milk the cows, Andy feeds the workhorses and cleans out their stalls.

7:30 a.m.
Andy washes his face and hands and changes his shirt for school. He eats a breakfast of ham, eggs, and biscuits.

8:30 a.m.

Andy attends a one-room schoolhouse. The teacher teaches one grade at a time while the others work on their lessons.

3:00 p.m.

Andy attends a blacksmithing class taught by the local blacksmith. He is learning to mold iron into various shapes. The WPA sponsors the class.

4:00 p.m.

Andy arrives home to help his uncle prepare for spring planting. Andy gathers loose rocks and mends a break in the fence.

5:00 p.m.

Andy helps his uncle and grandfather round up the cows for the second milking of the day. Then he cleans the barn.

6:30 p.m.

Andy and his family eat a supper of fried meat, beans, potatoes with onions, and lettuce with radishes grown on the farm.

7:30 p.m.

After a bath, Andy settles down to listen to the radio with his family. As he listens, his grandfather helps him mend his shoes with new soles and heels.

Why Do I Care?

The Great Depression ended many years ago. But that doesn't mean you can't find similarities between your life and the 1930s. How does the Great Depression affect your life today? Are there programs it led to that might not have existed otherwise? How might your life be different if the Great Depression had never happened? Use your imagination!

Dig Deeper

After reading this book, what questions do you still have about the Great Depression? Do you want to learn more about the New Deal? Or about daily life? Write down one or two questions that can guide you in doing research. With an adult's help, find a few reliable sources that can help answer your questions. Write a few sentences about how you did your research and what you learned from it.

Say What?

Studying the Great Depression can mean learning a lot of new vocabulary. Find five words in this book that you've never heard before. Use a dictionary to find out what they mean. Then write the meanings in your own words, and use each word in a new sentence.

Surprise Me

Chapter Five discusses daily life during the Great Depression. Learning about the Great Depression can be interesting and surprising. After reading this book, what two or three facts about the Great Depression did you find most surprising? Write a few sentences about each fact. Why did you find them surprising?

GLOSSARY

agencies
businesses or organizations with power to act for others

credit
money that a bank will allow a person to use and then pay back in the future with interest

crisis
a time of great danger or difficulty during which great changes take place

economy
the process by which goods and services are produced, sold, and bought in a country

folklore
the beliefs, legends, customs, and other traditions handed down from one generation to the next

grant
an amount of money that is given to someone by a government to be used for a particular purpose

inaugurated
to be placed in office with a ceremony

luxury
something that is not really needed but that gives pleasure, enjoyment, or comfort

prosecuting
holding a trial against a person accused of a crime to see if that person is guilty

topsoil
the upper layer of soil, in which plants have most of their roots

LEARN MORE

Books

Freedman, Russell. *Children of the Great Depression*. New York: Clarion Books, 2005.

Gunderson, Megan. *Franklin D. Roosevelt*. Minneapolis: Abdo Publishing, 2009.

Kyvig, David E. *Daily Life in the United States, 1920–1940: How Americans Lived Through the "Roaring Twenties" and the Great Depression*. Clermont, FL: Ivan R. Dee, 2010.

Websites

To learn more about Daily Life in US History, visit **booklinks.abdopublishing.com**. These links are routinely monitored and updated to provide the most current information available.

Visit **www.mycorelibrary.com** for free additional tools for teachers and students.

INDEX

ABOUT THE AUTHOR

Wendy H. Lanier is a former teacher who writes and speaks for children and adults. Recently, she also became a speech language pathologist. She and her husband of 26 years have three dogs, two daughters, and two granddaughters.